First Step Math

Circles

For a free color catalog describing Gareth Stevens' list of high-quality books, call 1-800-542-2595 (USA) or 1-800-461-9120 (Canada). Gareth Stevens' Fax: (414) 225-0377.

Library of Congress Cataloging-in-Publication Data

Griffiths, Rose.
    Circles/by Rose Griffiths; photographs by Peter Millard.
        p. cm. -- (First step math)
    Includes bibliographical references and index.
    ISBN 0-8368-1109-7
    1. Circle--Juvenile literature. [1. Circle. 2. Shape.
3. Geometry.] I. Millard, Peter, ill. II. Title. III. Series.
QA484.G75   1994
516.22--dc20   94-9592

This edition first published in 1994 by
Gareth Stevens Publishing
1555 North RiverCenter Drive, Suite 201
Milwaukee, Wisconsin 53212, USA

This edition © 1994 by Gareth Stevens, Inc. Original edition published in 1992 by A&C Black (Publishers) Ltd., 35 Bedford Row, London WC1R 4JH. © 1992 A&C Black (Publishers) Ltd. Additional end matter © 1994 by Gareth Stevens, Inc.

Series editor: Patricia Lantier-Sampon
Editorial assistants: Mary Dykstra, Diane Laska
Mathematics consultant: Mike Spooner

Printed in the United States of America
1 2 3 4 5 6 7 8 9 99 98 97 96 95 94

At this time, Gareth Stevens, Inc., does not use 100 percent recycled paper, although the paper used in our books does contain about 30 percent recycled fiber. This decision was made after a careful study of current recycling procedures revealed their dubious environmental benefits. We will continue to explore recycling options.

Circles

by Rose Griffiths
photographs by Peter Millard

Gareth Stevens Publishing
MILWAUKEE

How many circles have
you seen today?

There are circles all around us.

We made a collection of
circular objects.

6

I can make circles in this dough with a cookie cutter.

8

I can make circles by dropping a pebble into water.

Wheels are circular.
Kelly is making
trucks with wheels.

When I push this truck, it moves smoothly . . .

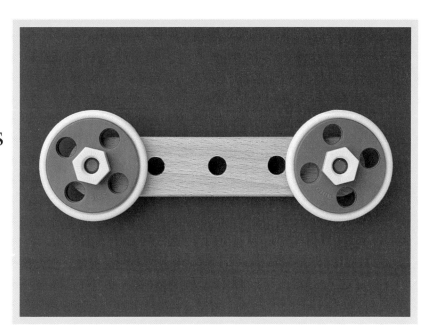

but this truck bumps up and down.

Can you see why?

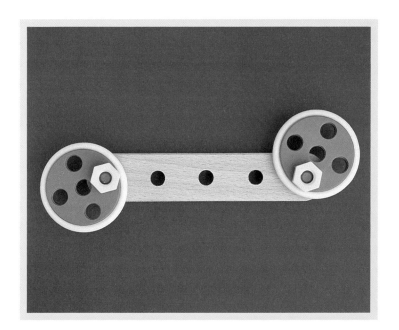

11

Jo is sketching something with circles.

Can you tell what it is?

Were you right?

My hoop is a circle.

When you look at a circle
from the side, it looks oval.

I'm drawing a circle with a safety compass.
How can I make a bigger circle?

How many circles have I drawn?

We are going to
draw a big circle.

This mark will be the
center of the circle.

Jo holds my jump
rope at the center.

We must keep the
rope pulled tight.

Sometimes we play games
in a big circle.

When we are in a big circle,
we can all see each other.

I'm printing with circles.

Do you like my hairy monster?

FOR MORE INFORMATION

Notes for Parents and Teachers

As you share this book with young readers, these notes may help you explain the mathematical principles behind the different activities.

pages 4, 5, 6, 7
Circles all around us

Each day, we see hundreds of circles. Encourage children to categorize the circles they find. For example, a pin head is a tiny circle, and a ferris wheel is a big circle. Some circles are just decorative, and some are useful. A circle is a two-dimensional shape; spheres and cylinders are three-dimensional shapes that have many circles on them.

pages 8, 9, 22-23, 24-25
Making circles

There are many ways of making circles that do not rely on drawing. Circles that share the same center are called concentric circles. For example, when you drop a stone in water, ripples move out from the center in a flowing, concentric pattern.

pages 10, 11 Wheels

Wheels run smoothly only when the axle is attached through the center of each wheel. This way, the distance from the axle to the ground remains the same.

pages 12, 13, 14, 15
Sketching circles

Young children need time and experience to understand how to represent a three-dimensional object as a two-dimensional drawing. This is a skill that needs practice. To help children draw in proportion, have them sketch circles freehand. Before sketching, it's helpful to talk about what the children can see. Encourage them to notice small details.

pages 18, 19, 20, 21
Drawing circles with a compass

The circumference is the distance all the way around a circle. The radius is the distance from a point anywhere on the outer edge of a circle to its center. The diameter is the longest measurable distance across a circle. It is twice the length of a radius and always passes through the center of the circle. Drawing a circle with a safety compass emphasizes the center and radius. Often, children mark a center that won't allow all the circle to fit on the page. Don't be tempted to step in before they see what happens. At first, talk about making bigger or smaller circles by altering the position of the arrow piece on the safety compass. Then talk about making the radius bigger or smaller, and if the child is ready, use specific measurements. Drawing a large circle (pages 20-21) also emphasizes the center and radius. The child who is drawing the circle must keep the rope taut so the colored marker is the same distance from the center all the time.

pages 24, 25 Printing circles

Encourage children to apply paint to the block with a brush rather than dipping the block into the paint. This helps the children concentrate longer on the shape of the circle.

Things to Do

1. Paper snowflakes

Trace a plate or other round object on a piece of white paper. Carefully cut out the circle, then fold it in half. Fold the paper in half two more times until you have a pie-shaped piece. Use scissors to cut small pieces out of the sides. Unfold your paper, and you will have a beautiful snowflake for decorating your room or windows.

2. Circle gift wrap

Design your own circle-print gift wrap or stationery. Use cross-sections of vegetables (such as carrots, cucumbers, or potatoes) as stamps. Apply colorful tempera paints to the vegetable stamp with a brush or dip your "stamp" into the paint before pressing it onto paper.

3. Circle magic

You can do a simple magic trick with two round coins of different sizes, such as a penny and a quarter. Trace the smaller coin on a piece of white paper. Fold the paper so the circle outline is folded in half, then cut out the inside of the circle. Place the larger coin inside the folded paper so it sticks out slightly. It will look as though the larger coin will not fit through. Bend the paper gently and push the quarter through the opening — the larger coin slips out easily!

4. Circle designs

Make personal, decorative patterns using circles of the same size. Then try making some designs with different-sized circles.

Fun Facts about Circles

1. If you fold a circle in half, the two sides always match.

2. Arctic musk oxen form a circle, facing outward, to protect their babies from enemies.

3. The Inuits of the Arctic outline a circle about 10 feet (3 meters) across before starting to build a round ice house, or igloo. When completed, the main part of an igloo is dome-shaped, like half of a ball.

4. The Equator is an imaginary circle that goes completely around the outside center of the Earth. The Equator falls at the exact midpoint between the North and South poles, and it is almost 25,000 miles (40,225 kilometers) long!

5. The people of the Zulu tribe of Africa live in straw huts built in the shape of beehives. These huts with circular windows are grouped together in a circular community, called a kraal, with cattle and other livestock living in the center.

6. The largest doughnut on record was 22 feet (7 m) in diameter. It was prepared in Florida in 1988.

7. Most coins are round and flat and made of copper, tin, nickel, or a combination of metals.

8. Stonehenge is a prehistoric monument in southern England made of huge stones, called monoliths, lined up in a circular pattern and surrounded by a circular ditch.

Glossary

center — the middle part or point of something.

circular — having a round or nearly round shape.

collection — a group of similar objects. You might have a collection of cards, stickers, stamps, plants, or some other object you may be interested in.

cutters — forms that are used to cut out a shape. For example, cookie cutters placed on and pressed into dough make decorative cookie shapes.

dough — a soft, thick blend of flour and liquids that is prepared for baking breads and other baked goods.

draw — to create a picture or likeness of something or someone by making lines on paper or some other surface.

hoop — a circular object that can be used as a toy.

oval — shaped like an egg.

pebbles — small stones or rocks.

press — to push into or against something.

print — to make letters or designs with ink or paint.

safety compass — a special tool with a safety feature used for drawing circles.

sketch — to make a rough, quick drawing of something or someone.

Places to Visit

Everything we do involves some basic mathematical principles. Listed below are a few museums that offer a variety of mathematical information and experiences. You may also be able to locate other museums in your area. Just remember: you don't always have to visit a museum to experience the wonders of mathematics. Math is everywhere!

The Smithsonian Institution
1000 Jefferson Drive SW
Washington, D.C. 20560

Museum of Science and Industry
57th Street and Lake Shore Drive
Chicago, IL 60637

Royal British Columbia Museum
675 Belleville Street
Victoria, British Columbia
V8V 1X4

Ontario Science Center
770 Don Mills Road
Don Mills, Ontario
M3C 1T3

More Books to Read

Circles
    Catherine Cheldrick Ross
    (Addison Wesley)

Leo Loves Round
    Eli Goldblatt
    (Harbinger House)

Fun with Sizes and Shapes
    J. Duddle
    (Childrens Press)

Round and Round and Round
    Tara Hoban
    (Greenwillow)

*Simple Science Experiments
   with Circles*
   E. Orii and M. Orii
   (Gareth Stevens)

What Shape?
   Debbie MacKinnon and
   Anthea Sieveking
   (Dial Books)

Videotapes

Clifford's Fun with Shapes
   (Scholastic)

Shapes and Colors
   (Bill Cosby's Picture Pages)

Index